NEW LIFE IN CHRIST

KERRI SLAUGHTER

NEW LIFE IN CHRIST:

Quick devotionals for busy people

TATE PUBLISHING
AND ENTERPRISES, LLC

New Life in Christ
Copyright © 2014 by Kerri Slaughter. All rights reserved.

No part of this publication may be reproduced, stored in a retrieval system or transmitted in any way by any means, electronic, mechanical, photocopy, recording or otherwise without the prior permission of the author except as provided by USA copyright law.

Scripture quotations are taken from the Holy Bible, King James Version, Cambridge, 1769. Used by permission. All rights reserved.

The opinions expressed by the author are not necessarily those of Tate Publishing, LLC.

Published by Tate Publishing & Enterprises, LLC
127 E. Trade Center Terrace | Mustang, Oklahoma 73064 USA
1.888.361.9473 | www.tatepublishing.com

Tate Publishing is committed to excellence in the publishing industry. The company reflects the philosophy established by the founders, based on Psalm 68:11,
"The Lord gave the word and great was the company of those who published it."

Book design copyright © 2014 by Tate Publishing, LLC. All rights reserved.
Cover design by Jim Villaflores
Interior design by Gram Telen

Published in the United States of America

ISBN: 978-1-63268-395-3
Religion / Devotional
14.07.29

I want to thank our Lord and Savior Jesus Christ. He has blessed me with the opportunity to write this devotional; without him, it would not have been possible. To Jesus be the glory! Special thank you to Billy and Cameron, you both have encouraged me to keep striving on no matter what. I love you both more than you'll ever know.

Introduction

This is a devotional book for anyone who desires to grow closer to Jesus Christ. The devotionals are quick to read and relevant to today's issues for many people. I hope this thirty-one–day devotional will help you each day.

"Draw nigh to God and He will draw nigh to you" (James 4:8).

Day 1

Trials Are a Blessing

Beloved, think it not strange concerning the fiery trial which is to try you, as though some strange thing happened unto you: But rejoice, inasmuch as ye are partakers of Christ's sufferings; that, when his glory shall be revealed, ye may be glad also with exceeding joy.

1 Peter 4:12-13

The Daily Devotion

God allows trials to come our way sometimes. Trials do one of two things: they either make or break us. Some people handle trials in a better way than others. For example, when faced with a trial, some will freak out and try to run the other way. On the other hand, others will pray to God for his guidance and help, ultimately trusting him to have his way. Trials are often seen as annoyances. However, a trial can be a blessing. You might be wondering, "How can a trial bless me?" A trial can be a blessing because it can make you grow in your walk with Jesus Christ. It also makes you stronger after you've persevered through to the end. Just as 1 Peter 4:13 tells us, "When we suffer through trials, we become partners with Christ." While trials are not easy, they will always be a thing that will happen at times. This is just a fact of life. However, you can choose to fight the good fight and let your trial bring you blessings or run in fear the other way. God will help you through any trial if you'll just ask him to.

PRAYER OF THE DAY

Father, we come to you and, first, thank you for your many blessings. You are a wonderful and awesome God, even through the trials we face. Trials are hard to go through, Lord, but thank you for always sticking by our side when we do have to endure them. Help us to remember that you are in control and things will work out for our best even if we don't understand the outcome immediately. Help us always to draw near to you, oh Lord, for you are our source of strength. Help us to be an encouragement to others as they face trials. In Jesus name we pray. Amen.

Jesus loves you.

Day 2

Qualities of People in the Last Days

This know also, that in the last days perilous times shall come. For men shall be lovers of their own selves, covetous, boasters, proud, blasphemers, disobedient to parents, unthankful, unholy, Without natural affection, trucebreakers, false accusers, incontinent, fierce, despisers of those that are good. Traitors, heady, highminded, lovers of pleasures more than lovers of God; Having a form of godliness, but denying the power thereof: from such turn away. For of this sort are they which creep into houses, and lead captive silly women laden with sins, led away with divers lusts, Ever learning, and never able to come to the knowledge of the truth.

2 Timothy 3:1–7

Kerri Slaughter

THE DAILY DEVOTION

The issue of when the last days will happen has been long debated. Some people say we are in them now while others think otherwise. Personally, I feel we are indeed in the last days. Too many things that were prophesied about in the Bible have happened. Today's verse names a lot of characteristics that people in the last days will portray. If we look around us, it is not hard at all to think of many people we have come in contact with who have one or more of these qualities. Characteristics such as these are not good to have. They are not from God. Instead, they are worldly ones that some have allowed to become a part of their life. The Bible warns us to stay away from people that posses these qualities. It is very important that we try our best to have godly friends and keep our guard up from adopting these bad habits. However, people that have these qualities need to be witnessed to about God's awesome love and forgiveness. God can still change people. We also need to earnestly pray for others as well as ourselves. The devil is hard at work separating people from God. This slimy one wants each person to share in his upcoming fate. Don't let him have the last laugh. Keep your guard up and pray for wisdom and strength to stay away from things that might persuade you to adopt these characteristics. Pray for the lost people in our world. I believe these are the last days, and things will only get worse if they are.

New Life in Christ

PRAYER OF THE DAY

Jesus, we come to you, and thank you for this day, Lord. You bless us in so many ways, far more than we can imagine. Lord, we look at the world around us, and it seems like we're living in the last days which the Bible speaks of. Lord, we live in a world that seems to get worse by the day. There is so much evil in it. Lord, help us to stay strong and avoid bad things. Help us to endure to the end and remind the devil of his fate. Help us to be a light for you to others. Lord, let those around us see that you are the *only way*. Speak to the hearts of those around us. We pray as you speak, oh, Lord, that people will open their hearts and ears. For we live in a world that so desperately needs you and your love. In Jesus name, we pray. Amen.

Jesus loves you.

Day 3

Confidence Comes from God

He trusted in the Lord God of Israel; so that after him was none like him among all the kings of Judah, nor any that were before him. For he clave to the Lord, and departed not from following him, but kept his commandments, which the Lord commanded Moses.

2 Kings 18:5–6

The Daily Devotion

Today's scripture shows us how Hezekiah trusted in the Lord. This was an example of the confidence that Hezekiah had in our Lord. How many people could honestly say that they trust God and place complete and utter confidence in him just as Hezekiah did? Probably not too many if people were honest with themselves. Placing confidence in God can sometimes be a hard thing to do. Our human nature wants to be in the know. This is how we are designed. However, God promises to work things out for good if we'll believe in him. Does this mean life will always go smoothly for us? No. But it does mean that God will use anything that the devil means for bad and turn it into his children's (who have accepted him as their Heavenly Father) favor. Confidence is something some of us have a lot of while others greatly lack this characteristic. However, God will help us in this if we'll just ask him to and sincerely let him. He still lets each person be the one to ultimately choose whether to place their confidence in him or not. Which choice will you make?

Prayer of the Day

God, we come to you and thank you for being God. Thank you that you are the One whom we can always depend upon to be there for us. Lord, we face so many struggles and upsets in this life. Life is so hard sometimes. We ask that you will give us the strength to endure and trust you to take care of things for us. You are the One who has the power, not us. We are weak, but you, oh, Lord, are very strong. Lord, when we are tempted to try and fix things ourselves without including you first, help us to remember to ask your input first. Lord, if the answer that you give us is not what we want to hear, help us to just trust you for you only do what is for our best. Help us to lean on you, our source of strength and rock. In Jesus name, we pray. Amen.

Jesus loves you.

Day 4

Your Thankfulness Brings Praise to God

And he took him by the right hand, and lifted him up: and immediately his feet and ankle bones received strength. And he leaping up stood, and walked, and entered with them into the temple, walking, and leaping, and praising God. And all the people saw him walking and praising God: And they knew that it was he which sat for alms at the Beautiful gate of the temple: and they were filled with wonder and amazement at that which had happened unto him. And as the lame man which was healed held Peter and John, all the people ran together unto them in the porch that is called Solomon's, greatly wondering.

Acts 3:7-11

The Daily Devotion

No doubt that the man in this scripture was thankful to God for making him able to walk. In fact, he was so thankful that he "started walking as well as jumping and praising God" (Acts 3:8). Like the man in today's scripture, we all have things to be thankful to God for. We all should give God the thanks and glory every day for his many blessings upon us. You may not think that you're blessed, but you definitely are. You may look around and see others who seem to be more blessed than you, but you're blessed. Everyone should always make it a point to thank God. When you thank God, it brings him glory. I encourage and challenge you to thank God every day for his many blessings. If you're not thankful for the things he gives you, then he might just take them away.

PRAYER

Lord, we come to you and thank you for your many blessings upon us. Lord, we are so blessed. We sometimes fail to see it, but you bless us each day with breaths to take, food to eat, and a place to sleep. You bless us so much that we can't even comprehend it all. Help us to always to have humble hearts. In Jesus name, we pray. Amen.

Jesus loves you.

Day 5

Tossed by the Wind

> If any of you lack wisdom, let him ask of God, that giveth to all men liberally, and upbraideth not; and it shall be given him. But let him ask in faith, nothing wavering. For he that wavereth is like a wave of the sea driven with the wind and tossed.
>
> James 1:5–6

The Daily Devotion

Most people do not have trouble when it comes to asking God for things. Usually, most people have trouble believing that God will provide what's best after they ask. Some will believe that God will answer their prayer for a while and then lose their faith. Scripture tells us that "nothing should be wavering with our faith" (James 1:6). We shouldn't go back and forth in it all the time, but rather be more constant. Sometimes, it is hard to have faith; it really is. That is why we should pray and ask God to help us trust in him. God always answers our prayers; it may not be in the way that we want, but he does answer them. I encourage and challenge you to not waver in your faith. Please don't let the wind toss you around. May God bless you.

PRAYER

Lord, we come to you and thank you first and foremost for all of the blessings that you so freely and lovingly bestow upon us. Lord, the Bible tells us that you desire for us to have faith. But, Jesus, that is sometimes so hard to do. There are times when our faith seems to be on a see-saw. We are sorry for this. Help us, oh, Lord, to have the faith that we need at all times. Help us to have the unwavering faith like you want us to have. Help us to trust you at all times for you will always be there with us. In Jesus name, we pray. Amen.

Jesus loves you.

Day 6

The Bible Can Guide Your Life

Open thou mine eyes, that I may behold wondrous things out of thy law. I am a stranger in the earth: hide not thy commandments from me. My soul breaketh for the longing that it hath unto thy judgments at all times.

Psalm 119:18–20

The Daily Devotion

Do you read your Bible? If you do read it, do you ask God to open your eyes to what he wants you to learn? The Bible is God's Word for us. I've heard it said that Bible spelled out would stand for, "Basic Instructions Before Leaving Earth." I like this saying because the Bible is full of instructions for us. Plus, it offers comfort and encouragement for us as well as many other things. The Bible is a great tool to guide us in our everyday lives. Sadly, a lot of people let their Bibles collect dust because they never open them. Some people have a Bible just to say that they have one, not to read it. If we will allow it to though, the Bible can really help us by guiding us in life as well as many other areas. However, we have to read it before it can help us. If we never read the Bible, how are we to know what all it says? God doesn't want our Bible to sit on a shelf somewhere and collect dust. If that was the case, he wouldn't have let it be written. I encourage and challenge you to read your Bible and ask God to allow its words to guide you in your everyday life. You will find that you're blessed if you do. God bless.

Prayer

Lord, we come to you and thank you for everything that you do for us. We don't deserve your blessings, but you so freely give them to us anyways. Lord, thank you for giving us your Holy Word, the Bible. God, we often get so busy with our day-to-day activities that we sometimes forget to read your Word and spend time with you. We are so sorry for this. Please forgive us. The busyness of life makes us sometimes forget that you are supposed to be number 1 every single day. God, please also forgive us when we're so tired that our time with you is cut short and not the quality time that you deserve. Help us to make quality time every day to spend reading your Holy Word. Our Bibles are not meant to collect dust. Help us to apply your principles to our lives daily. In Jesus name, we pray. Amen.

Jesus loves you.

Day 7

Always Be Thankful

Rejoice evermore. Pray without ceasing. In every thing give thanks: for this is the will of God in Christ Jesus concerning you.

1 Thessalonians 5:16–18

The Daily Devotion

We live in a world today that is very ungrateful. Sadly, many people forget to say thank you when you do something nice for them. Even sadder is the fact that people forget to say thank you to God. Today's scripture tells us to always give thanks in all circumstances. Some people don't have much trouble with saying thank you to God when things are going good. However, when things get to going bad, saying thanks is the last thing on their mind. When bad things happen, it is hard to be thankful, but this is what we're supposed to do. We need to ask God to help us be thankful for our many blessings. There are plenty of things that we should thank God for. If you wake up every morning, you should thank God. If you have breath to breathe, you should thank God. If you have a roof over your head and food to eat, you have something to be thankful for. I encourage and challenge you to make it a habit of thanking God for his many blessings. You may not feel like saying thank you, but please humble yourself and say it. Please don't fall into the world's trap of thinking that you deserve the things you've got and become ungrateful. If you're not thankful for the blessings that God gives, he can easily take them away. God bless you.

PRAYER

Lord, we come to you and thank you for your many blessings. You bless us with so much, Lord, far more than we deserve. Lord, please forgive us for the times when we have failed to thank you. Help us to always have a thankful and humble heart. Help us to be appreciative of the things we have. In Jesus name, we pray. Amen.

Jesus loves you.

Day 8

Praise God for Everything

> Every day will I bless thee; and I will praise thy name for ever and ever.
>
> Great is the Lord, and greatly to be praised; and his greatness is unsearchable.
>
> One generation shall praise thy works to another, and shall declare thy mighty acts.
>
> I will speak of the glorious honour of thy majesty, and of thy wondrous works.
>
> Psalm 145:2–5

The Daily Devotion

Some days, I like to wake up early in the morning and just watch the sunrise with a cup of coffee in my hand. I enjoy listening to the birds. When I'm riding a jet airplane, I enjoy just looking out the window and seeing the clouds. I love to spend time with my husband and my son; we don't have to be doing anything, I just love the time we have together. What I just told you is just a few things that I thank God for. I want everyone who is reading this to get up early one morning and enjoy the sunrise. Listen to the birds sing and tell God thank you for allowing me to be alive to see this. Sometime in the day, turn that TV off, spend time with your kids, and thank God for that time because they will grow up. If your kids are grown up, then call them up and tell them you love them. Thank God for them. If you don't have kids, then spend time with your family and enjoy it. Strive to watch less TV, spend less time on the computer, and all the other stuff that's out there. Enjoy the simple things in life; you will be thankful you did. God bless.

Prayer

Lord, we thank you for your many blessings upon us. Lord, we often get caught up in the many things of this life. Most of the things that we spend our free time on are just distractions. Please forgive us where we fail. Help us to realize the things that are truly important in life. Help us to learn to recognize the things that are distractions. Help us to enjoy the simple life and many blessings that you so freely give us. Also, oh, Lord, help us to spend time with you and our families. You bless us with our family for only a short period of time. Help us to enjoy the time we have with them instead of the pleasures of this world. In Jesus name, we pray. Amen.

Jesus loves you.

DAY 9

QUARRELS

But foolish and unlearned questions avoid, knowing that they do gender strifes. And the servant of the Lord must not strive; but be gentle unto all men, apt to teach, patient.

2 Timothy 2:23–24

THE DAILY DEVOTION

Every one of us is guilty of having at least one quarrel during our lifetime. We are only human. However, having a quarrel with someone is not a very good thing. Have you ever stopped and just thought about how stupid some arguments are? Some arguments really are petty and silly. While it is in our human nature to argue why our side is better at times, we should strive to stay away from this. Most of the time, having an argument with someone does not produce any good. Rather, it produces much harm. Oftentimes, arguments result in hurt feelings, resentment, or both. Words that shouldn't have been spoken are. Once a harsh word is spoken, you cannot take it back. The ability for someone to forget harsh things you say to them is not very easy. Sadly, this is a fact that people tend to forget until after the damage has already taken place. I encourage and challenge you to pray and ask God to help you refrain from arguments and quarrels. Ask God to help you have the ability to bite your tongue, if you have to! God bless.

Prayer

God, we come to you and thank you for your abundant blessings upon each of us. Lord, we ask you to forgive us when we fail you. Lord, our worldly nature sometimes takes control and we get involved in arguments, which result in people getting hurt. We lose the willpower to control our tongue. Lord, we humbly ask that you will help us to stay away from silly and unnecessary arguments. Helps us to easily distinguish between those things that we should take a stand for and those that are better left alone. Help us to make amends with those that we have hurt with our words or actions. Help us to shine your awesome light. In Jesus name, we pray. Amen.

Jesus loves you.

DAY 10

YOUR DAILY LIFE

And that ye study to be quiet, and to do your own business, and to work with your own hands, as we commanded you; That ye may walk honestly toward them that are without, and that ye may have lack of nothing.

1 Thessalonians 4:11–12

THE DAILY DEVOTION

If someone asked you what your daily life is like, how would you respond? Would you answer honestly or lie? Could you honestly say that you lead a quiet life and stay out of others' business? A lot of people could not say this if they were honest. We live in a society where it seems like many people know everything about your life. Today's scripture tells us that we are supposed to "live quiet lives and mind our own business" (1 Thessalonians 4:11). This is very hard for a lot of people to do. Just about everywhere you go, even to the local supermarket, you hear gossip about someone. While gossip is usually juicy, we are not supposed to do this. If you gossip about someone, word will eventually get back to them. This may not happen in the immediate, but it will. Today's scripture also tells people that they "should work with their hands" (1 Thessalonians 4:12). We live in an economy where jobs are scarce. Many people have lost their jobs in recent years and have great difficulty in finding another one. This is definitely a sad situation. On the other hand, there are people that just will not work because of laziness. First, it should be stated that people who have a physical or mental illness, which significantly disables them, are not lazy as some people assert. However, true laziness does exist in able-bodied people that simply refuse to work. If someone will not work just because they are lazy, then they develop idle hands. The Bible clearly tells us not to have "idle hands" (Proverbs 10:4). Do you use your hands to work or let them be idle? I encourage and challenge you to ask God to help you lead a quiet life that is free from the massive amounts of gossip circulating throughout society. Also, humbly ask him to help you never have idle hands. God answers our prayers, but in his perfect timing and way if we have faith. God bless.

PRAYER

Lord, I come to you and thank you for this glorious day. I ask that you will help me to be quiet when someone treats me wrong or gossips. Help me to be the person that will bring you the glory and honor that you deserve. It is my prayer that when people see me they will see you. In Jesus name, I pray. Amen.

Jesus loves you.

Day 11

No Wrong Makes a Right

But he that doeth wrong shall receive for the wrong
which he hath done: and there is no respect of persons.

Colossians 3:25

The Daily Devotion

Today's scripture shows us that when someone does wrong, that they will be paid back for doing that wrong. There is no exception to this. It does not matter what your last name is, how much money you have, how popular you are, etc., if you do wrong, you will be repaid for it. A lot of people think that when someone does them wrong that they should repay them. People think that revenge is sweet. Revenge is not sweet though. It may be sweet in the immediate, but that sweetness will definitely turn sour quickly. No matter how bad you want revenge on someone, doing someone wrong in return does not make things right. You've probably heard the phrase, "Two wrongs don't make a right." There is a lot of truth in this phrase. Jesus told us that we should turn the other cheek when we're done wrong. Often, this is hard to do. Our human nature wants to get even. However, it is important to keep in mind that even though it may be painful to overlook a wrong, Jesus will help you if you'll just ask him to. We should forgive those that do us wrong. No one said that forgiving someone would be an easy thing to do. In fact, it can be quite difficult. Many people have the misconception that forgiving someone is basically approving of their ways. It is just the opposite. Forgiveness means that you choose to accept the fact that someone wronged you, choose to turn it over to God rather than harbor resentment and attempting to get revenge, and love that person anyway. I encourage and challenge you to not repay someone when they do you wrong and be quick to truly forgive. Ask God to help you. God bless.

Prayer

Lord, help me to strive to be like you today. Help me to treat others the way I want them to treat me. I pray for your mercy and love to fall down on me. In Jesus name, I pray. Amen.

Jesus loves you.

Day 12

Please God, Not Men

> But as we were allowed of God to be put in trust with the gospel, even so we speak; not as pleasing men, but God, which trieth our hearts.
>
> 1 Thessalonians 2:4 (KJV)

The Daily Devotion

Many men and women in our world today work quite hard to please other people. We live in a society that promotes keeping up with those that are wealthy or have many possessions. Sadly, this vast amount of worrying about what others think of them causes men and women to lose focus on what really matters, what God thinks. Each one of us is guilty of being a people pleaser at some point in our lives. Being a people pleaser can be physically and emotionally draining. So why do we do it? There are different reasons why people try to be a people pleaser. Sometimes, the motivation for being a people pleaser comes from fear of rejection or desiring to have a better lifestyle. However, today's scripture shows us how we should please God and not man. A person's opinion of you can change at any time for any given reason. But God knows your heart and will always be there for you, even when you disappoint him. Oftentimes, when you disappoint a person, they don't want anything to do with you for a while. This is not so with God. I encourage and challenge you to try and be a God pleaser. Try not to care so much about whether people are pleased with you or not. God's opinion of you is the one that really matters. God bless you.

PRAYER

Lord Jesus, help us to please you and not man. Help us to do what you have called us to do no matter what man thinks. Forgive us for trying to please man instead of you. In Jesus name, we pray. Amen.

Jesus loves you.

Day 13

The Real Test

Thou shalt not hearken unto the words of that prophet, or that dreamer of dreams: for the LORD your God proveth you, to know whether ye love the LORD your God with all your heart and with all your soul.

Deuteronomy 13:3

The Daily Devotion

Today's scripture tells us that God "tests us to see if we love Him with all of our heart and soul" (Deuteronomy 13:3). It is easy for some to say that they love God. Some people even say that they love God with all of their heart and soul. This is great if it's a completely honest response. However, many times, it is not completely true. Honestly loving God with every fiber in your being means different things to each person. But one universally common trait of loving him this much is displayed in a person's priorities. If a person truly loves God this much, he will be their number

1 priority in life. God knows our heart. He knows every thought that we have. He knows exactly how much we love him. So fooling him is not possible! One reason why he might test a person's heart is to clearly show him or her just how much love that he or she really has for him. This testing from God is very real. Nothing about God's tests are jokes. Therefore, people need to take it seriously. There is so much going on from day to day. However, we need to make sure that God is our number 1. If he's not, then we have tragically missed the point. I encourage and challenge each of you to examine your heart and see if you really love God as much as you think. If you see that he's not your number 1, then please make him so ASAP. You won't regret making him number 1. God bless.

Prayer

Lord, I pray that I will pass all of the tests that you have for me no matter what they may be. Help me to be the person that you have called me to be. In Jesus name, I pray. Amen.

Jesus loves you.

Day 14

Don't Discourage Your Kids

Fathers, provoke not your children to anger, lest they be discouraged.

Colossians 3:21

The Daily Devotion

It is easy to become discouraged in our world today. There is so much meanness. Lots of people struggle just to make ends meet. When adults become discouraged, it is easy to pass that onto kids. Tragically though, when men and women pass frustrations and discouragement onto their kids, it is done so in the form of anger, snappiness, and harsh words. Actions such as this are not something that people of any age desire, including kids. Many people try to act like kids are not smart. However, this is not the case. Kids are very smart. They pick up on the least little thing.

If you're discouraged, it would be extremely easy to pass that on to them with your attitude. Likewise, if you are frustrated, those feelings are all too easy to pass on with the tone of your voice and choice of words. Colossians 3:21 instructs us "not to provoke our kids because of making them discouraged." Lots of parents provoke their kids either intentionally or not. This is something that people need to work on. Parents are supposed to encourage their kids, not do the opposite. If you spent your childhood being discouraged, chances are that your adult years will be the same. This is not a good situation. Therefore, we should strive to lift our kids up. Help to start them off on the right foot. I encourage and challenge you to carefully watch yourself that you don't discourage your kids. Pray and ask God to help you encourage your children instead of discourage them. Kids are truly a tremendous blessing from God. Treat your children like the wonderful blessing from God that they are. God bless.

PRAYER

Lord Jesus, we come and ask you to help us to be the parents that you want us to be. When we have to discipline our kids, help us to do it with love and not with a spirit of anger. Lord, we also ask that you help us to remember that they are only human when they do make a mistake. Help us, Lord, to love our kids no matter what they do and always remember that they are a blessing from you. Help us to show our kids the way to you in Jesus name, we pray. Amen.

Jesus loves you.

Day 15

Run from Temptation

But thou, O man of God, flee these things; and follow after righteousness, godliness, faith, love, patience, meekness. Fight the good fight of faith, lay hold on eternal life, whereunto thou art also called, and hast professed a good profession before many witnesses.

1 Timothy 6:11–12

The Daily Devotion

Temptation is everywhere you look. We live in a world that doesn't put God first or many who even believe in him. Lots of people sin like there's no tomorrow with little or no thought to the consequences. The devil is out there "like a roaring lion trying to devour" (1 Peter 5:8) us. He knows that our human bodies get weak sometimes. Because he is sneaky and just plain evil, he uses this against us to try and make us sin. If we sin, we are pulling away from God. This is exactly what the devil wants. However, while the devil may throw everything at us to try and tempt us, we have a choice. We can stand strong and rely on God's strength to avoid the temptation, or we can give in and sin, leaving the consequences for later. The right thing to do is to run from temptation when it comes knocking on your door. Temptation always has and always will be a part of life. It was with Adam and Eve in the Garden of Eden and it will be with you throughout your life as well. However, I urge you to stand strong against it. Fight the good fight. Ask God to help you resist temptation, for it is only by his perfect strength that you can be successful.

Prayer

Lord, we come to you and thank you for your many blessings upon us. Thank you, Lord, for this day and night. Lord, there is so much temptation out there. Everywhere we look, temptation of some sort is out there trying to lure us in to sin. We ask, oh, Lord, that you will help us to stand strong when we are faced with temptation. Help us to run the other way. Help us to rely on your strength to make it through. Please forgive us when we are weak and give in to sin. For we give you all the honor, praise, and glory forever. In Jesus precious name, we pray. Amen.

Jesus loves you.

Day 16

Never Put Money Above God

> Lay not up for yourselves treasures upon earth, where moth and rust doth corrupt, and where thieves break through and steal.
>
> Matthew 6:19

The Daily Devotion

A lot of people in our world today have a deep desire for money. Naturally, it takes money in order to live from day to day. However, many people have a huge desire for more money other than to just meet basic living needs. Sadly, many develop such a love for money that they turn into greedy people. Today's scripture tells us not to store up treasures on earth. We are all guilty of doing this, if we're honest. Each one of us has a collection of some sort or something that we spend a great deal of money on. This is a natural characteristic that all humans possess. However, sometimes people take this to the extreme. It should be said that God is not against us having things. However, it does become sin if we place anything above him. This includes the "love of money" (1 Timothy 6:10). Someday, we will all die. The Bible promises us this. When we do die, we cannot take any of our money or possessions with us. There are some people that don't really understand this and instead hold the misconception that their stuff can go with them. Just as we came into the world with no worldly possession, we will leave in the same manner. There will always be many people who are greedy and put their love of money above God, which is not a good thing. The Bible instructs us in Exodus 34:14 against putting other things or people above God. Each one of us is supposed to have God as number 1 in our lives (Mark 12:30). Many things that we encounter during our lives will try and distract us from putting God first, with the desire for money being the top distracter. I encourage and challenge you not to put anything or anyone ahead of God in your life. Money will come and go, but God is there to stay. God bless.

PRAYER

Lord, help me to be content with what I have. Help me, Lord, to never put money first. The true treasure I have is you, oh, Lord. Please forgive me for the times when I place money ahead of you. In Jesus name, I pray. Amen.

Jesus loves you.

Day 17

Trust Christ Without Doubting

And it came to pass, when Jesus had made an end of commanding his twelve disciples, he departed thence to teach and to preach in their cities. Now when John had heard in the prison the works of Christ, he sent two of his disciples, And said unto him, Art thou he that should come, or do we look for another? Jesus answered and said unto them, Go and shew John again those things which ye do hear and see: The blind receive their sight, and the lame walk, the lepers are cleansed, and the deaf hear, the dead are raised up, and the poor have the gospel preached to them. And blessed is he, whosoever shall not be offended in me.

Matthew 11:1–6

The Daily Devotion

Jesus performed many miracles while he walked on this earth. He still performs miracles today. Sadly, many people doubt him. The above verse tells us how Jesus replied in response to John's question. Every day, Jesus blesses each of us in many different ways. Often, we do not recognize our blessings, much less thank God for them. Many people have an easier time trusting Jesus when things are going good versus when things get difficult. When things start getting hard, that is when we really need to trust Jesus—even trust him the most. Jesus will never leave nor forsake us (Joshua 1:15), so why doubt him? Why do people doubt his ability to take care of us? Lots of people do not like having to trust because it requires that you have faith. Faith is believing when you can't see. Jesus will *always* take care and provide for you. He has never left you hanging, and he's not going to start now. So why doubt him? I encourage and challenge you to believe in Jesus and not doubt him. May you have a blessed day.

Prayer

Lord, forgive me for having doubts sometimes. Help me to trust you all the time. Thank you for the things you are going to do today. I know you have something big in store for me today. I know that you have someone that you will put in my path. I pray that you will give me the right words to say to those you place in my path. I pray this in Jesus name. Amen.

Jesus loves you.

Day 18

Judgment Seat of Christ

> Therefore we are always confident, knowing that, whilst we are at home in the body, we are absent from the Lord:
>
> (For we walk by faith, not by sight:) We are confident, I say, and willing rather to be absent from the body, and to be present with the Lord. Wherefore we labour, that, whether present or absent, we may be accepted of him. For we must all appear before the judgment seat of Christ; that every one may receive the things done in his body, according to that he hath done, whether it be good or bad.
>
> 2 Corinthians 5:6–10

The Daily Devotion

The Bible tells us that each and "every one of us will be judged someday by God" (2 Corinthians 5:10). There is no escaping this. The latter part of 2 Corinthians 5:10 goes on to tell us that we will be judged "for the things we do while we're on this earth." This includes those good and bad things that we do. God's judgment is "always just and fair" (Psalm 19:9). Some people try to say that God is not fair by using the excuse that "it's their life and they should get to do what they want when they want without being judged." Every person has the right to do what they want. God does *not* force himself upon you. However, whether you do good or bad, you will still be judged come judgment day. He is your Heavenly Father no matter what, whether you ever accept him into your heart or not. Are you prepared come judgment day? If you've accepted Jesus into your heart, you will have an eternal home with Jesus; you won't receive the punishment we all (if we're honest) deserve. If you haven't accepted Christ into your heart, then I encourage and challenge you to do so ASAP. The result of your judgment depends on it. God bless.

Prayer

Lord Jesus, I ask you that you will pour out your love on me and help me to tell others about you. Help me to tell the lost with a loving attitude that we all will have to face the judgment seat of Christ. I ask that when the lost see me, they will see you Jesus. In Jesus name, I pray. Amen.

Jesus loves you.

Day 19

True Champion

> I have fought a good fight, I have finished my course,
> I have kept the faith.
>
> 2 Timothy 4:7

The Daily Devotion

Super Bowl Sunday has become a huge tradition for many people in our world. Millions or perhaps billions of people just throughout the United States tune into this game. No matter which two teams compete against each other, only one team can be called the champion. While everybody wants their team to be the winner, there is One who always wins: Jesus. Jesus has already defeated everything and everyone possible. He won the victory on the old rugged cross so many years ago. This victory can never be taken away. Many won't acknowledge that his victory is all that really matters. Champions on his side will, though.

If you have accepted Christ as your Savior, then that makes you a champion too. If not, won't you give him your heart today? He is waiting for you with arms stretched open. Just like a quarterback often waits too late to throw the ball and loses the opportunity to get a touchdown, don't let your chance pass you by.

PRAYER

Lord, we come to you and thank you for your many blessings upon us. Lord, you bless us so much more than we deserve. Thank you, Jesus, for being the one true champion. Help us, Lord, to remember that you are what really matters and not get caught up in things that distract us from you. May you help us to show others the right way. Help us to fight the good fight and finish our race. In Jesus name, we pray. Amen.

Jesus loves you.

Day 20

Description of Real Love

Charity suffereth long, and is kind; charity envieth not; charity vaunteth not itself, is not puffed up, Doth not behave itself unseemly, seeketh not her own, is not easily provoked, thinketh no evil; Rejoiceth not in iniquity, but rejoiceth in the truth; Beareth all things, believeth all things, hopeth all things, endureth all things. Charity never faileth: but whether there be prophecies, they shall fail; whether there be tongues, they shall cease; whether there be knowledge, it shall vanish away.

1 Corinthians 13:4–8

The Daily Devotion

This is a popular Bible verse that many believers and unbelievers both know. Many people choose to use this passage for their wedding vows. 1 Corinthians 13 is known as the love chapter of the Bible—and it is. Verses 4–8 tell us perfectly what real love is. Real love is not based upon lust.

However, a lot of people confuse lust with real love. God made true love far more special for each of us than lust; it goes way beyond that. Lust is short-lived while true love lasts. While verses 4–8 tell us how we should love others, it also goes beyond that. This is how God loves each of us. His love is the perfect and lasting love that we all need. Many probably don't think about this as being a description of how God loves us when they read this passage. With this in mind, I encourage and challenge you to give this passage some serious thought. Is the Bible's description of real true love the same as yours, or is yours based upon how the world defines it? If your definition isn't the same as what the Bible says, I pray that you will pray and ask God to help you change your view of what true love really is. God bless.

PRAYER

Lord, I pray that you will show me today what real love is all about and help me to get through this day with a godly attitude. If I see someone today that is rude to me and talks in an unpleasant manner, help me, Lord, to have a godly attitude toward them, an attitude that shows love and mercy. In Jesus name, I pray. Amen.

Jesus loves you.

DAY 21

COMFORT

Blessed be God, even the Father of our Lord Jesus Christ, the Father of mercies, and the God of all comfort; Who comforteth us in all our tribulation, that we may be able to comfort them which are in any trouble, by the comfort wherewith we ourselves are comforted of God. For as the sufferings of Christ abound in us, so our consolation also aboundeth by Christ. And whether we be afflicted, it is for your consolation and salvation, which is effectual in the enduring of the same sufferings which we also suffer: or whether we be comforted, it is for your consolation and salvation. And our hope of you is stedfast, knowing, that as ye are partakers of the sufferings, so shall ye be also of the consolation.

2 Corinthians 1:3–7

THE DAILY DEVOTION

Many people believe that when God comforts us, our hardships go away. If that were so, people would turn to

God only to be relieved of pain and not out of love for him. Real comfort can also mean receiving the strength to deal with our hardships. The more we suffer, the more comfort God gives us. If you're feeling overwhelmed, allow God to comfort you. Remember, every trial you endure will later become an opportunity to help someone who suffers a similar hardship. God bless.

Prayer

Our Father which art in heaven, Hallowed be Thy name. Thy kingdom come. Thy will be done in earth as it is in heaven. Give us this day our daily bread. And forgive us our debts, As we forgive our debtors. And lead us not into temptation, But deliver us from evil. For Thine is the kingdom and the power and the glory forever. Amen.

Matthew 6:9–13

Jesus loves you.

Day 22

Welcoming Children Is Welcoming Christ

And he took a child, and set him in the midst of them: and when he had taken him in his arms, he said unto them, Whosoever shall receive one of such children in my name, receiveth me: and whosoever shall receive me, receiveth not me, but him that sent me.

Mark 9:36–37

The Daily Devotion

Today's scripture is Jesus words speaking to each of us. Jesus is telling us that if anyone "welcomes a child in His name, then that person welcomes Him" (Mark 9:37). Jesus has a great love for children. There are several examples of this in the New Testament such as Jesus talking to the children. Loving children comes natural to some people while others have to put forth more effort to do so. However, we are called to love everyone (John 13:34–35) which includes children too. When you welcome a child in Jesus name, then you are doing what is right. We should all want to welcome Jesus. I encourage and challenge you to welcome Jesus. If you haven't welcomed him into your life, please do so immediately. There are severe consequences (Matthew 7:21–23) if you don't welcome Jesus into your heart. Please make things right with God before it's too late, if you haven't already. One is not promised another minute or even second for that matter. God bless.

PRAYER

Lord, help me to always love kids the way you want me too. When my child sees me, I pray that they will see you in me. Help me to be there for them. In Jesus name, I pray. Amen.

Jesus loves you.

Day 23

Greed

> He coveteth greedily all the day long: but the righteous giveth and spareth not.
>
> Proverbs 21:26

The Daily Devotion

Merriam-Webster's dictionary defines *greed* as "a selfish and excessive desire for more of something (as money) than is needed."[1] When someone mentions the subject of greed, most are quick to associate this with money. While greed can come in the form of money, it also arises in many other areas as well. Areas such as your time are not commonly thought of when talking about greed. The majority of people are super busy from day to day. People rush to get things done before the day's end with little to no thought about God. Sure, some people sneak in five minutes of alone time with God before rushing to do something recreational. There is nothing wrong with having clean fun. However, if you are spending an hour doing something fun and only five minutes with God daily, then something is wrong. Sadly, too many people are greedy with their time for God. God just gets the minimum time to keep one's conscience at bay. Our day-to-day life is not supposed to be this way. It should be of utter importance to give God all of us, not just a tiny fraction. God doesn't expect you not to have fun. But he would like more of your time than just the minimum. Are you being greedy with your time with God? If so, tomorrow is a new day. Ask for his help to re-prioritize.

Prayer

Lord, we come to you and thank you for your many blessings. Lord, forgive us for the times when we have been greedy with our time. We know that you are supposed to be number one in our life. Sometimes, our selfish desires cloud our judgment. Help us to do better and spend adequate time with you. In Jesus name, we pray. Amen.

Jesus loves you.

"Greed." Merriam-Webster.com. Accessed April 10, 2014. http://www.merriam-webster.com/dictionary/greed.

Day 24

Hide and Seek

> For mine eyes are upon all their ways: they are not hid from my face, neither is their iniquity hid from mine eyes.
>
> Jeremiah 16:17

The Daily Devotion

Most small children think that if they can't see you, then you can't see them. The people of Judah may have wished that hiding from God was as simple as closing their eyes. Although they closed their eyes to their wrongs, everything was revealed to God. Have you ever been tempted to play hide-and-seek with God, thinking that maybe he won't notice a certain action? But God knows absolutely everything. You may be able to hide things from man, but it is impossible to hide anything from God. So instead of trying to hide something from God, why not seek him? God bless.

Prayer

Lord, we come to you and thank you for your many blessings upon us. Help us to always be grateful for your blessings both big and small. Lord, sometimes we let our sinful selves get the best of us and think that we can hide it from you. Please forgive us for this, Lord. Nothing in this entire world can be kept from you for you know everything. Help us to always seek the narrow path for it leads to life in you. Help us to be a light unto others. In Jesus name, we pray. Amen.

Jesus loves you.

Day 25

Enjoy Life

He maketh me to lie down in green pastures: he leadeth me beside the still waters.

Psalm 23:2

The Daily Devotion

The day started out really good. I got up out of the bed, had my coffee, and some breakfast. I have a sickness that affects my energy level, but I don't let it get the best of me. My husband, son, and I had some quality family time together watching a movie. Times like this really mean a lot to me. Creating good memories with your loved ones is important. God gave our loved ones to us to spend time together. Sadly, a lot of people do not spend much time with their loved ones. They let their circumstances get in the way. God wants us to have some enjoyment in our lives, though. Life can be stressful. Spending some quality time with our family can sure make your stresses disappear for awhile. So make sure to schedule some quality time with your loved ones. Rest in the Lord, and enjoy life no matter what happens. You'll be glad that you did. God bless.

Prayer

Lord, help us to spend time with you and our loved ones because there is no promise for tomorrow. Just help us to enjoy life. Enjoy all the birds singing, the sunrise and sunset, and everything that life has to offer. Thank you, Jesus, for loving us so much that you died for us and you rose again. Help us to tell people about you. In Jesus name, we pray. Amen.

Jesus loves you.

Day 26

Abortion

Then the word of the Lord came unto me, saying, Before I formed thee in the belly I knew thee; and before thou camest forth out of the womb I sanctified thee, and I ordained thee a prophet unto the nations.

Jeremiah 1:4–5

The Daily Devotion

The issue of abortion is a touchy subject for many people. Many people have some kind of connection with abortion in one way or another. For example, you might know someone who had an abortion, someone who was almost aborted, someone thinking about having an abortion, etc. Whatever the reason, the issue of abortion is a scary thing. God tells us in Jeremiah 1:4-5 that "before I formed thee in the belly I knew thee." This means that before a baby is even conceived, God knows that baby closely. Some people do not think that God cares about babies, but his word tells us otherwise. There are various reasons why a woman would choose to have an abortion. A person might think that abortion is the only answer for them, but that's the devil telling that person a lie. There are always options other than abortion. If you can't take care of a baby for whatever reason, then why not give that baby up for adoption? Thousands of couples are waiting to adopt a child. Please give that unborn child a chance at life. I am not here to judge anyone who has had an abortion for it is not my place to judge. If you have had an abortion, then I pray that you have forgiven yourself and asked God's forgiveness. God will forgive you if you'll just sincerely ask him to. He is a loving God that cares for you. A good movie that everyone should watch is called *October Baby*. *October Baby* (2011, Samuel Goldwyn Films & Provident Films) is about the issue of abortion. Lastly, if you know someone who is thinking about having an abortion, pray for them. God still answers prayers—perhaps not in the way that we want, but in the best way.

PRAYER

God, we come to you and thank you for your many blessings. Thank you for the gift of life. Lord, help us not to take the gift of life for granted. So many people do take life for granted. Help us all to understand just how much that you value our life. Help us to make the right choices in our lives. Help us to pray for others who we see are struggling. In Jesus name, we pray. Amen.

Jesus loves you.

Day 27

Happy

But let the righteous be glad; let them rejoice before God: yea, let them exceedingly rejoice.

Psalm 68:3

The Daily Devotion

Being happy sometimes isn't easy. In fact, when life is difficult, being happy is one of the hardest things in life. When you wake up every day, get down on your knees and tell God to make you happy! There is much in life to be happy with. Jesus blesses us all with so much. A lot of people choose not to be happy because they do not have all of the material possessions that are desired. Some material possessions are nice to have, but all of that will not make you happy; only Jesus will make you happy. If you don't have Jesus in your heart, then ask him to come to your heart and you will have a lot to be happy for. See, God has blessed you so much that you don't really think about it. He has blessed many of us with a husband or wife and kids. Also, most of us have a home to go to or a job. God wants you to be happy in life. Things can always be much worse. But thank God for what you have. Be happy in Christ. Every day, tell your spouse, your kids, and people who are in your life that you love them. Lastly, don't ever take anything for granted. Put Jesus number 1 in your life. You will not go wrong. God bless.

Prayer

Our Father which art in heaven, Hallowed be Thy name. Thy kingdom come. Thy will be done In earth as it is in heaven. Give us this day our daily bread. And forgive us our debts, As we forgive our debtors. And lead us not into temptation, But deliver us from evil. For Thine is the kingdom and the power and the glory forever. Amen.

Matthew 6:9–13

Jesus loves you.

Day 28

No Worries

Be careful for nothing; but in every thing by prayer and supplication with thanksgiving let your requests be made known unto God. And the peace of God, which passeth all understanding, shall keep your hearts and minds through Christ Jesus. Finally, brethren, whatsoever things are true, whatsoever things are honest, whatsoever things are just, whatsoever things are pure, whatsoever things are lovely, whatsoever things are of good report; if there be any virtue, and if there be any praise, think on these things. Those things, which ye have both learned, and received, and heard, and seen in me, do: and the God of peace shall be with you.

Philippians 4:6–9

The Daily Devotion

Today's verses deal with the issue of worrying. The Bible tells us not to be "anxious about anything but in prayer"

(Philippians 4:6). After this verse, the Bible goes on to tell us that "God will give us peace" (Philippians 4:9). Worrying is a part of life for many of us. Some people worry a lot while others have a carefree approach to life. Those that tend to worry need to remember that the Bible calls on us to give our worries to God instead of trying to handle them ourselves. This is not always easy to do because the devil wants you to worry instead of trusting God. The devil will throw all kinds of tricks your way to make you worry. But when he does throw temptation your way, stand strong in God. God will help you through whatever your situation is. May God bless you.

PRAYER

Jesus, we come to you and thank you for this day. Jesus, you know that worrying is a part of our lives sometimes. We know that you want us to turn our worries over to you when struggles come our way. We admit that it is hard for us to do this at times. We humbly pray that you will help us learn to trust you to handle our worries and give us the peace from it all. May your love and peace abound over us. In Jesus name. Amen.

Jesus loves you.

Day 29

Don't Speak in Anger

Even so the tongue is a little member, and boasteth great things. Behold, how great a matter a little fire kindleth! And the tongue is a fire, a world of iniquity: so is the tongue among our members, that it defileth the whole body, and setteth on fire the course of nature; and it is set on fire of hell.

James 3:5–6

The Daily Devotion

Anger is a very common trait that many people possess in our world today. More and more people, for various reasons, let their anger get the best of them. Regretfully, when someone allows their anger to get the best of him or her, it causes major problems. When a person loses his or her temper, those around are directly affected, not only the person whom you lose your temper with, but anyone else that hears (such as a child). Have you ever stopped and thought about that? If a man loses his temper with his wife in front of their child, then the child will also be affected. James 3:6 tells us that "the tongue is a fire and evil." When we speak in anger we are doing evil. When we allow our tempers to get the best of us, then that is doing evil. The tongue can be used for good and not evil. However, it takes a lot of prayer, reading the Bible, and dedication to use it for good. With the world in such horrible shape as it is today, it's very tempting to speak in anger. It doesn't help that the devil constantly tries to tempt us to be displeasing to God. I encourage and challenge you to not give into the temptation of speaking in anger. Ask God to help you stay calm when issues arise. Ask him to help you stay calm toward life's pressures and troubles. Here's a tip, when you feel yourself getting angry, stop and say a quick prayer (even if silently), and take a slow deep breath. May God bless you.

Prayer

Lord, help me not to speak in anger to anyone. Help me to have a peaceful spirit that will be full of mercy and love. I pray this in Jesus name. Amen.

Jesus loves you.

Day 30

Closer

O God, thou art my God; early will I seek thee: my soul thirsteth for thee, my flesh longeth for thee in a dry and thirsty land, where no water is.

Psalm 63:1

The Daily Devotion

Many people have the wrong idea about how a personal relationship with God is supposed to be. Sadly, many people think that going to church every now and then is what constitutes a personal relationship with God. This could not be further from the truth! God wants to have a close, intimate relationship with everyone each day, not just a few minutes of your time every few months or so. As Christians, it is supposed to be our utmost desire to want to spend time with our Lord Jesus. Remember back when you were dating your spouse and had those feelings, "I can't live without him/her"? Well, this is how we should feel about God. We should feel as if it's impossible to go one day without having fellowship with Jesus. After all, he is our Source of existence. Where do you invest your time: with God or elsewhere? We're all human and have had times when God was pushed to the back burner. The good thing though is that we serve a mighty God that is full of love and forgiveness. Life gets busy, but there is always a few moments that can be spared for our Savior Jesus Christ if you'll just honestly seek him. Please don't ignore him any longer. He's lovingly waiting to spend time with you. God bless.

Prayer

Lord, we come to you and thank you for your many blessings upon each of us. Lord, we ask for forgiveness. There have been times when we didn't seek to be as close to you as we should have. We have put other things before you, and we are sorry for this. Help us to always put you number 1. Help us always to desire your fellowship, for it is because of you that we are alive. Help us to draw others to you. In Jesus name, we pray. Amen.

Jesus loves you.

Day 31

True Enjoyment in Life

There is nothing better for a man, than that he should eat and drink, and that he should make his soul enjoy good in his labour. This also I saw, that it was from the hand of God. For who can eat, or who else can hasten hereunto, more than I? For God giveth to a man that is good in his sight wisdom, and knowledge, and joy: but to the sinner he giveth travail, to gather and to heap up, that he may give to him that is good before God. This also is vanity and vexation of spirit.

Ecclesiastes 2:24–26

The Daily Devotion

Is Solomon recommending that we party until we drop? No, he is encouraging us to take pleasure in what we're doing now and to enjoy life because it comes from God's hand. True enjoyment in life comes only as we follow God's guidelines for living. Those who really know how to enjoy life are the ones who consider each day to be a gift from

God, thanking him for it and serving him in it. That's what you do, right? Live your life for God. Enjoy the sunrise, sunset, birds singing, and things like that. God bless.

PRAYER

God, thank you for all your abundant blessings. Life is so busy at times, Lord, that we get stressed out and forget to enjoy the blessings that you so freely give us. Help us to slow down and enjoy the simple things in life. In Jesus name, we pray. Amen.

Jesus loves you.